TABLE OF CONTENTS

Introduction	page 2
What Is Your Vision For Your Life?	pages 3 - 9
See Yourself As A Goal-Winner	pages 10 - 21
When You Wake Up, Get Up	pages 22 - 27
Life Is Not A Game, It Is Serious	pages 28 - 34
Everyone Wants Success and Happiness	pages 35 - 40
Deep Breath, Now Focus	pages 41 - 46
Revise Like The Greatest Student In The World	pages 47 - 53
Read Something New Every Day	pages 54 - 59
Always Be Learning	pages 60 68
Don't Act Like An Idiot	pages 69 - 73
What I Wish I Knew When I Was Your Age	pages 74 - 80
A New You	pages 81 - 85
Get A Great Night's Sleep	pages 86 - 91
Final Thoughts	pages 92 - 97
Notes & Doodles	pages 98 - 101
About The Author	pages 102 - 103
Other Great Books For Your Library	page 104
A Public Thank You	pages 105 - 110

DESIGN YOUR LIFE - DESIGN YOUR FUTURE

"This book will guide, inspire and motivate students to become the greatest students in the world. There are no limits to what you can achieve or how far you can go if you become 'The Greatest Student in The World'."

Richard Whitaker

WHAT IS YOUR VISION FOR YOUR LIFE?

WHAT IS YOUR VISION FOR YOUR LIFE?

- What do you envision for your future? What career do you aspire to? Where do you see yourself living? What car do you desire to own? What style of clothing do you wish to wear? But above all, what kind of individual do you aspire to become?

- You can start today; please don't put it off until tomorrow. We all know that tomorrow will soon become today again, and if we keep postponing, the task will never get done.

- To begin, get a large sheet of paper and start writing all your ambitions and desires for your life. This practice can be an excellent way to get your brain into thinking about your personal goals. Now, start to write down your goals with precision on the paper. Take the time to determine precisely what you aspire to achieve, record it, and subsequently decide on how to make it a reality.

WHAT IS YOUR VISION FOR YOUR LIFE?

- There are two main reasons why it is crucial to write down your goals. 1. Remembrance: By putting your goals on paper, you ensure that you won't forget them. This serves as a helpful reminder of what you're working towards and keeps your objectives fresh in your mind. 2. Activation: Writing down your goals jumpstarts your thinking process. It engages your imagination and motivates you to take action. By putting pen to paper, you are actively committing yourself to pursue your goals and take the necessary steps to achieve them.

- Design your affirmation cards. Write these as if they have already happened. For example. "I am so happy and grateful now that I have achieved the grades I needed and I feel fantastic". As well as this, how about some mantras; consider this; "Today is going to be an amazing day, and at the end of this amazing day, I am one step closer to reaching my goal".

WHAT IS YOUR VISION FOR YOUR LIFE?

- Write down what you need to do to achieve your goals as well as any obstacles you may come across on your journey.

- Creating a list of individuals who can provide support in your journey towards achieving your goals is essential. These individuals can include your family members, friends, and teachers. By sharing your goals with these people, you can hold yourself accountable and receive the necessary encouragement to keep going, especially during times when you feel tired and lack motivation.

- When you realise that you have approximately 15 minutes left before your tea, football practice, or dancing lesson, look for an activity that can be completed in about 10 minutes. Choose something that moves you closer to your goals.

WHAT IS YOUR VISION FOR YOUR LIFE?

- Ensure that you take action every day to achieve your goals. Begin each day by jotting down your goals and identifying three specific tasks you can accomplish to make progress towards them.

- When you have goals and you check something off your list for the day, you will feel amazing, happy, and full of energy. Reward yourself; you deserve it.

- Set aside a few moments twice a day to close your eyes and engage in the following visualisation exercise. Imagine that you have successfully achieved one of your personal goals. Take note of the emotions and sensations that arise during this exercise. Reflect on the following questions: How does achieving your goal make you feel? Can you describe the sense of accomplishment and joy that comes with success? Now, take that positive energy and motivation with you as you go out there and enjoy the rest of your day.

WHAT IS YOUR VISION FOR YOUR LIFE?

- Start writing your life vision in the 'Life Vision Cloud' below; what will your life look like?

WHAT IS YOUR VISION FOR YOUR LIFE?

- Do not simply talk about your vision and goals; take action towards them every day until you achieve those goals.

- To help you stay on track with your goals, you will need to keep focussing on your vision and remind yourself every single day about your life vision. Remember, this is why you are working so hard every day.

- Wake up each day with a purpose and a passion so that you realise that you are one day closer to achieving your goals.

SEE YOURSELF AS A GOAL-WINNER

SEE YOURSELF AS A GOAL-WINNER

- Having goals gives you a purpose. Waking up in the morning and going to school, college or university becomes an exciting opportunity when you have clear goals in life. Start your day by eagerly jumping out of bed, ready to make the most of it.

- The reason we set goals is to give us something to aim for. Goals allow us to focus and keep pursuing in the right direction. You can't hit a goal that you cannot see.

- If you don't have goals, how will you know what direction to take or if you're succeeding or falling behind in life? Having a goal provides clarity on your progress and the path you're taking.

- Every day, visualise that you have already achieved your goals and relish in this success. You will feel incredible. Take a moment, close your eyes, and let your emotions run wild.

SEE YOURSELF AS A GOAL-WINNER

- When you write down your goals, you are reprogramming your subconscious mind to start identifying as being a goal-setter and goal-achiever. Here are a couple of examples of goals you can write down: "I will dedicate more time to revising this week." An even more clear and precise goal would be to write; "I will commit to revising for 10 minutes every morning, right after breakfast."

- If you don't have a goal, you will likely end up working for someone who does have a goal, and all you will end up doing is helping them achieve and fulfill theirs.

- Without goals, you will not reach your desired destination. However, when you set specific goals, you have the power to accomplish anything you desire.

- A goal is a dream with a specific date attached to it, which transforms it into a credible reality.

SEE YOURSELF AS A GOAL-WINNER

- What is your motivation? Why do you wake up in the morning? I'm not just talking about attending your school, college, or university. What are your ultimate objectives in life? If you desire, you can take one step closer to those objectives every day.

- Your long-term thinking improves your short-term decision-making. By consistently considering your goals and envisioning the life you desire for your future, the choices you make today will become much simpler.

- I don't always enjoy getting up at five o'clock each morning; sometimes, it can be difficult. However, I have developed the habit and achieved the goal that I set for myself, so I continue to do it.

- Always remember, it is not the goal itself that is important; it is who you become as you pursue your goal.

SEE YOURSELF AS A GOAL-WINNER

- Successful people achieve success because they set goals; they have a clear vision of what they want to accomplish and can describe the path they need to take to get there. Therefore, if you desire success and happiness, it is so important to establish goals that serve as targets to strive for. It is impossible to reach a goal that does not exist.

- Find somewhere quiet and be alone for a while. Then, grab a large piece of paper and start jotting down all the things you desire for your future. Feel a sense of excitement as you do this; write them down as if you are creating a shopping list. Now, go out and live your best life. Strive for a good life, a happy life, and a successful life. Don't wait any longer. Start pursuing it right now.

SEE YOURSELF AS A GOAL-WINNER

- it is so important to write down your goals; 5 magical things happen when you do:

1. You send a message to your brain saying: 'This is important, because I am taking the time to write it down'.
2. You say the words to yourself.
3. You hear the words as you are saying them.
4. You can see the goals on paper
5. Finally, because you have wrote it down, you can see it; it becomes 100% real.

Remember to state your why and write down your tactics, eg) what are you going to do in order to achieve your goal. Finally, when will you achieve this goal.

SEE YOURSELF AS A GOAL-WINNER

- Having goals and planning for your future is like stepping into the future. It helps bring the future into the present so you can take action now. What an incredible opportunity that is.

- It is important to add a why to your goals. Answer the following questions:

- Why do you want to achieve them?

- What difference will it make to your life?

- How will it affect you and other people in your life?

SEE YOURSELF AS A GOAL-WINNER

Goal Example **Why? Tactics and Achieved by...**

Achieve a Grade 7 in my Physics Exam

So I can get onto the college course I desire to be on.

Revise for one hour each morning when I wake up.
Attempt 3 exam questions every evening.

By 22nd August 2024

Now write it in the present and be proud of it:

It is August 22nd and I have achieved my grade 7 in Physics. I am a superstar and feel fantastic and can now get on to the course I worked so hard for."

SEE YOURSELF AS A GOAL-WINNER

Goal 1 **Why? Tactics and Achieved by...**

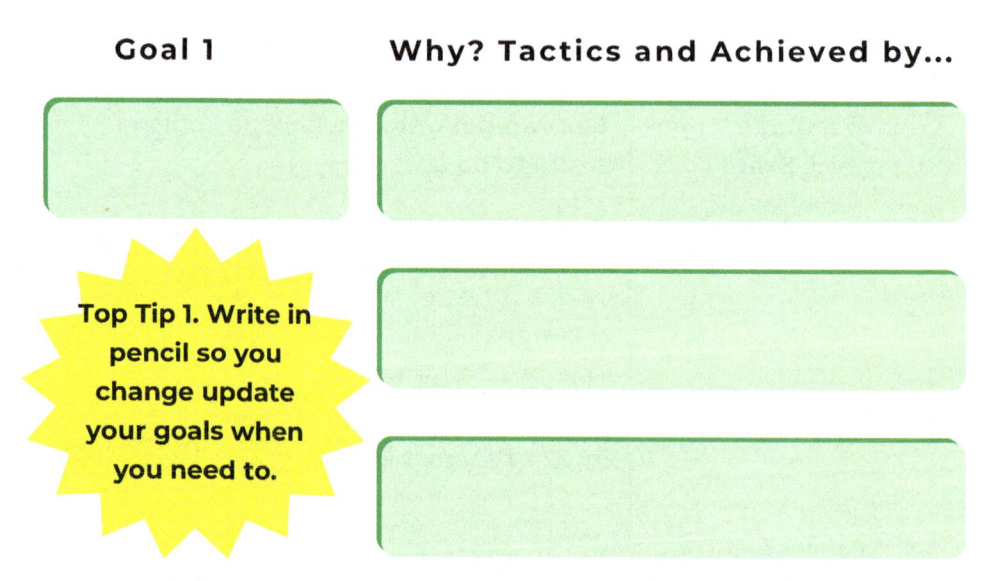

Top Tip 1. Write in pencil so you change update your goals when you need to.

Now write your goals in the present, as if you have already achieved them and be proud of it:

SEE YOURSELF AS A GOAL-WINNER

Goal 2 **Why? Tactics and Achieved by...**

Top Tip 2. Remember to write your goals down in the present tense too.

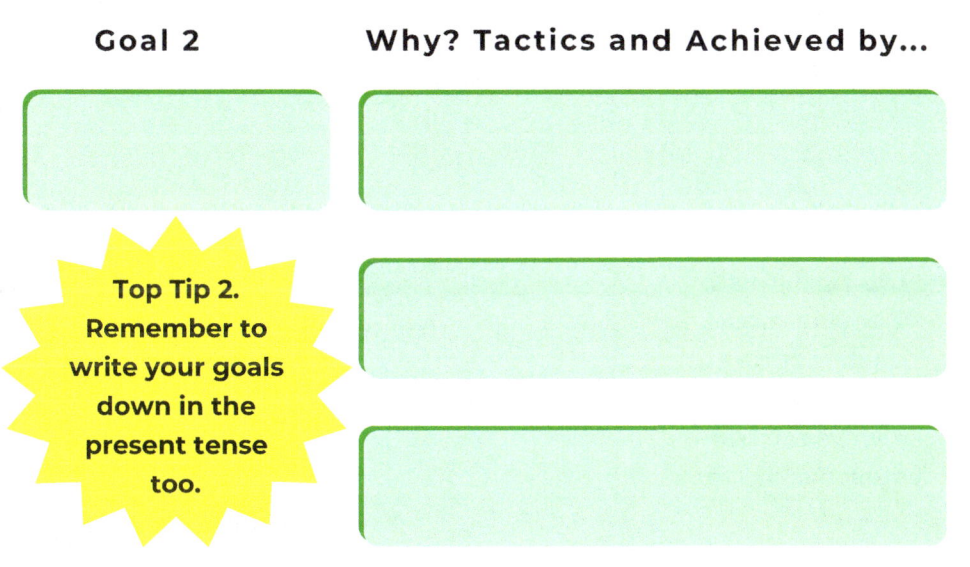

Now write your goals in the present, as if you have already achieved them and be proud of it:

SEE YOURSELF AS A GOAL-WINNER

Goal 3 **Why? Tactics and Achieved by...**

Top Tip 3. Read them out aloud each morning and every night. Always remind yourself of them.

Now write your goals in the present, as if you have already achieved them and be proud of it:

SEE YOURSELF AS A GOAL-WINNER

"YOU GOT THIS"

WHEN YOU WAKE UP, GET UP

WHEN YOU WAKE UP, GET UP

- When you wake up, immediately get out of bed. Avoid wasting time lying under the covers and resist the temptation to hit the snooze button on your alarm. Taking this winner's approach in the morning will set the tone for a fantastic, positive, and productive day.

- Start your day early and enjoy your morning. There is nothing worse than waking up late and putting yourself under unnecessary pressure, rushing around, and causing undue stress. Allow yourself plenty of time to focus on self-care and relaxation.

- Don't spend your morning obsessing over other people on social media; prioritise yourself. Giving too much attention to others will prevent you from concentrating on what truly matters; yourself, the most significant person in the world.

WHEN YOU WAKE UP, GET UP

- **Stretch and exercise:** Engaging in stretching and exercise activities in the morning can help you wake up effectively, raise your heart rate, and release endorphins. These hormones are known to lower stress levels and increase your overall sense of well-being.

- **Start your day with a healthy, nourishing breakfast** that will provide you with long-lasting energy. Include a serving of fresh fruit in your morning meal, add protein and good carbohydrates to your breakfast to enhance concentration and increase energy levels.

- **Wash yourself and clean your teeth every morning,** not just when you can be bothered, but every single morning. You can't just tell yourself that you will do it twice as long tonight, it doesn't work like that.

WHEN YOU WAKE UP, GET UP

- Read something motivational each morning; this will help you get psyched up for the day and give you an additional energy boost.

- Look at yourself in the mirror, smile, and tell yourself how amazing you are. Remind yourself that you are about to have a phenomenal day.

- Dress smart, look smart. Let the whole world know that you mean business and are ready to take on whatever life throws at you.

- Rewrite your goals every morning so you can remind yourself why you are getting up and going to school, college, or university. This will help you remember the reasons you are studying so hard and reassure you that all your efforts will be worthwhile in the end. You'll know that your hard work will lead to success and happiness.

WHEN YOU WAKE UP, GET UP

- Start your day by setting off early each morning, giving yourself ample time to reach your destination. Take away all the stress and worry of being late.

- Use your travel time productively. Take advantage of your commute in a car or on a bus or train as an opportunity to engage in educational or motivational activities. When possible, opt for listening to or reading something educational. This could include audiobooks; including this one of course, podcasts, or any form of reading about the topics you are currently learning about. Prepare ahead of time by selecting educational resources that you can easily access during your commute. This enables you to make the most of your travel time. Actively engage with the material by taking notes, reflecting on key points, or brainstorming ideas related to the topic.

WHEN YOU WAKE UP, GET UP

- Make it your goal to bring a smile to people's faces through your words and actions. Remember that a smile can be contagious, especially when you are the one responsible for putting it there.

- When you prioritise self-care and dedicate the first hour of each morning to personal growth and well-being, the benefits are immense. By "investing in you," you will experience increased energy levels, enhanced productivity, and a boost in self-esteem. Remember, taking care of yourself sets the tone for the rest of the day.

LIFE IS NOT A GAME, IT IS SERIOUS

LIFE ISN'T A GAME, IT IS SERIOUS

- Enhancing your vocal communication skills is essential because when you open your mouth, you are revealing your true self to the world. Take the opportunity to express how incredible you are and demonstrate the kind of person you are. This will greatly benefit you in all parts of your life, making it easier, happier, and ultimately more successful.

- When you notice someone who appears sad, upset, or uncomfortable, why not support them? Whether it's being there for them, lending an ear to listen, or offering them a comforting presence. Remember that everyone experiences unhappiness from time to time, and we all shed tears. By bringing joy to someone's life, you not only contribute to their happiness but also improve your well-being, creating a positive environment for everyone.

LIFE ISN'T A GAME, IT IS SERIOUS

- **It doesn't matter whether you like the subject you are studying or not, or if you get along with the person sitting next to you in class or the teacher in front of you. You still must do the very best you can, with no excuses, because it will impact your future. Don't let others influence your future and therefore *your* happiness and *your* success.**

- **Don't just have a wish or a hope about what your future will be like; have a strong desire. What exactly do you want? When you know, go get it with both hands.**

- **Don't let the time-wasters and losers waste your time, or you could become a loser just like them. Why would you let these people potentially affect your future for the worse? Don't let them ruin your future happiness and success; it makes no sense at all, and you probably won't even associate with them in your later life anyway.**

LIFE ISN'T A GAME, IT IS SERIOUS

- Treat yourself as amazingly as possible, and you will build a fantastic relationship with yourself. By mastering this approach, you will experience increased happiness and a greater sense of fulfillment.

- Stay away from drama queens and negativity kings. They will only bring you down and negatively impact your life. Don't allow them to drag you down to their level. Instead, surround yourself with happy and positive individuals. You'll be amazed at how much better you'll feel and how much happier you'll become.

- Limit your time on social media. Focus on yourself, as you are the important one and the star of your own movie. Don't feed into others' egos, but nurture your own and practice self-love.

LIFE ISN'T A GAME, IT IS SERIOUS

- Don't be a TikTok Top Banana, a WhatsApp Warrior, a Snapchat Scaramouche, or an Instagram Immortal. Instead, if you are bored or have some spare time, read a book, go for a walk, drop down and do some push-ups, or do some revision. Do something that will better yourself, add value to your life, and not just entertain yourself needlessly.

- Make every year of your education count, regardless of the number of years you have left - whether it's 1, 2, 3, 4, 5, or more. Don't waste your time in education. Since you attend anyway, aim to give your best effort. Your future self is depending on you.

- When you write something down, a message is sent to your brain, reminding you of its importance. Therefore, it is crucial to jot down all the key points during lessons and independent learning to ensure retention and understanding.

LIFE ISN'T A GAME, IT IS SERIOUS

- Identify the students in your year group who consistently achieve excellent results in their assessments and ask them about their study methods. How do they prepare for exams? How frequently do they revise? What subjects do they focus on when studying? What they tell you will be extremely valuable. Pay attention to their advice and take action based on their suggestions, and you too can experience similar academic success.

- If you want to be popular, be nice and kind to people. If you want to be disliked, unpopular and have very few friends, then act foolishly or unwisely. So, it's obvious, isn't it? Choose not to be foolish.

- Don't complain about things that have happened to you; the world is not against you. If something is bothering you, take action and choose to smile while taking positive steps forward.

LIFE ISN'T A GAME, IT IS SERIOUS

- You can always predict your future, it is simple, just look at how you are acting each day. What are you doing? How hard are you working towards your goals? How are you treating other people? Want a great future? Then you know what to do.

- When you are happy, you bring joy to the people around you, which in turn brings more happiness to yourself, creating an overall atmosphere of happiness. It is truly a wonderful feeling."

EVERYONE WANTS SUCCESS AND HAPPINESS

EVERYONE WANTS SUCCESS AND HAPPINESS

- Everyone wants to be successful; deep down, no one wants to be unsuccessful in life.

- Unsuccessful individuals often make excuses such as "I'll start tomorrow." Let's not fall into that mindset. Start taking action today, no matter how small the step may seem. Whether it's improving your physical health or expanding your knowledge, commit to go for a walk or engage in study sessions today. Remember, every effort counts towards your journey to success.

- Success is simple, just find out what other successful people do and do what they do, until you get the same results. Everyone, once upon a time was in your position; everyone has to start somewhere. All inventions, all successes, all happiness came from an idea. Whta is your idea?

EVERYONE WANTS SUCCESS AND HAPPINESS

- The person you will become in the future will be determined by everything you do today. So, what do you want your future to look like? Do you want to be happy, successful, and have great friends, or unhappy, unsuccessful, and lonely? If you have answered that question honestly, then seriously think about how you will act today.

- It is not the goals you set that make you successful; it is the person you become while working towards your goals. This includes the skills you learn, the knowledge you gain, the discipline you require, and the attitude you possess.

- You won't get roses if you plant dandelion seeds. So, if you want success, plant successful thoughts inside your head, and you *will* achieve success.

EVERYONE WANTS SUCCESS AND HAPPINESS

- Successful people learn every single day. You need to ask yourself, every single day, "What can I do today, to better myself?" Some of the most successful and richest people on the planet have been quoted saying; that if they had just one superpower, they would choose the ability to be able to read quicker.

- If you see yourself as successful, happy, and motivated, you will inevitably achieve more success, happiness, and peak performance. Why? Because your thoughts shape your reality, and by focusing on positive outcomes, you attract and manifest them in your life. You become what you think about most of the time.

- The key to success is self-discipline. This means doing what you should do when you need to do it, even when you don't want to do it. So, just do it.

EVERYONE WANTS SUCCESS AND HAPPINESS

- It is not enough to just be cool at school; you need to work hard to become successful. Once you achieve success, then you can truly be cool.

- Did you know that you have the ability to make choices that can determine if you will be healthy or unhealthy, successful or unsuccessful, rich or poor, happy or unhappy, hardworking or lazy? These choices are simple, but they can have a profound impact on your life.

- It takes 5 to 7 years to become excellent at any particular pastime. Start now, start today, so you can become better sooner. The time will pass anyway, so do you want to be brilliant and ultimately successful, or just average?

EVERYONE WANTS SUCCESS AND HAPPINESS

- To achieve success, instead of wishing for things to be easier, strive to improve yourself. Merely wishing won't lead you anywhere, so dedicate yourself to hard work every day. As you become better, you'll find that the work becomes easier.

- All achievements, all riches, and all successes have a beginning. So, when are you going to start?

- Don't wait for that special day; exam results day, when you receive your envelope with your final exam grades inside and become upset because you didn't get the grades you needed as you didn't put in the effort. Put in the effort every single day and you will achieve the grades you deserve, attain success in life, and find the happiness we all seek.

DEEP BREATH,
NOW FOCUS

DEEP BREATH, NOW FOCUS

- **It is crucial to prioritise your sleep and aim for an adequate amount of rest every night. Experts recommend getting between 8 and 10 hours of sleep to ensure optimal functioning. Failing to get enough sleep can result in fatigue and hurt your ability to focus and concentrate effectively. Prioritise your well-being by making sleep a priority.**

- **Indulge in Brain Food. It is important to nourish our brains with healthy foods, such as fruits and vegetables. However, it is always a good idea to do your research and choose the ones that you not only enjoy and like to eat but also which fulfil your own dietary needs.**

- **Stretch and Exercise: This will improve blood flow, not just to the body but also to your brain.**

DEEP BREATH, NOW FOCUS

- Diaphragmatic breathing is a helpful technique to reduce stress and anxiety. You can use this technique when you feel overwhelmed or anxious, such as before an exam. Find a quiet place where you can sit down and relax.

Here are the steps to practice diaphragmatic breathing:
1. Sit with your back straight.
2. Breathe in through your nose for 4 seconds.
3. Exhale slowly through your mouth for 6 seconds.
4. Repeat this process 10 times.

Practicing diaphragmatic breathing can have several benefits:
1. Improves focus and concentration.
2. Promotes relaxation.
3. Reduces stress levels.
4. Increases oxygen supply to the brain.

DEEP BREATH, NOW FOCUS

- Focus on one task at a time. If a distracting thought or idea comes to mind, jot it down and address it later. Stay committed to your main objective and don't let these thoughts divert your attention.

- Establish a Routine: Create a consistent schedule for yourself. Once you have determined what tasks need to be completed, follow through and complete them accordingly. By having a set plan in place, you will enhance your brain's ability to concentrate on the task at hand.

- Avoid all distractions. Find a quiet space and leave your phone in another room. If you minimise or eliminate distractions, you will be able to fully focus and concentrate on what is important.

DEEP BREATH, NOW FOCUS

- At the beginning of your revision session, establish a goal and commit to accomplishing it. Determine the duration of your revision session. Identify the specific objectives you aim to achieve during this session. Outline the subject matter or topics you plan to revise.

- Study in small blocks, starting with 10 minutes and then taking a break. If 10 minutes is too long to start with, you can begin with 5 minutes.

- Revise with the best students, those who consistently achieve good scores or grades in their assessments. These students exhibit a strong desire to succeed and actively work towards excellence. Their admirable mindset will positively influence you, encouraging you to become a dedicated and focused individual in your work.

DEEP BREATH, NOW FOCUS

- Make time for family and loved ones. This will remind you of the important things in life and give you time for fun, pleasure, and rewards.

- Please make sure to drink plenty of water throughout the day. It is advised to carry a water bottle with you at all times, especially when you need to concentrate on a task. Staying properly hydrated will help keep your brain functioning at its best.

- Remind yourself of your life vision. If you have a vision of what you want your life to look like, this will serve as a reminder of why you need to stay focussed on your work.

REVISE LIKE THE GREATEST STUDENT IN THE WORLD

REVISE LIKE THE GREATEST STUDENT IN THE WORLD

- Revision can initially be challenging, so it is essential to establish a routine of picking up a revision guide and just start reading, even if just one paragraph. Taking small steps will help train your brain. Remember, it takes time, so don't fret over it. Eventually, this practice will become a valuable habit; a habit that brings remarkable results.

- Do some revision each morning, even if it's just for five minutes. This will set you up to have a fantastic start to an amazing, productive day and get your brain in the right frame of mind.

- Research tells us that it takes about six minutes to shift your attention back to your revision after looking at your phone. Therefore, it is advisable to put your phone away while you are revising.

REVISE LIKE THE GREATEST STUDENT IN THE WORLD

- Purchase a cheap stopwatch for your revision sessions. When setting a specific amount of time, such as blocks of 25 minutes, use the stopwatch instead of your phone. We're all aware that phones tend to be a distraction.

- Whenever possible, find a quiet and peaceful environment where you can focus on revising. If you don't have a suitable space at home, consider asking your school, college, or university if they have a designated study area. Additionally, you might have a friend or family member who would be willing to offer you a space. Being away from distractions will greatly benefit your learning.

- Begin your revision sessions slightly earlier each evening and extend them slightly later. However, remember to work efficiently to maximise productivity.

REVISE LIKE THE GREATEST STUDENT IN THE WORLD

- **When producing revision posters; lettering in large bubble writing and colouring it in with pretty colours is nice to do for some, but is it important? Will it help you pass your exams? Focus on the important things. If needs be, produce a template on your computer and then print lots out. Then you aren't wasting valuable revision time.**

- **Repetition is key. Do something often enough and your brain will learn it. So, when you are learning a new topic, keep doing it, keep practicing key questions until you understand it and that skill will then stay with you forever. Yes, it may take longer for some to grasp an idea or develop a particular skill or talent than it does for others, but DO NOT let that stop you. You will get it in the end, just have faith and keep at it.**

REVISE LIKE THE GREATEST STUDENT IN THE WORLD

- If it helps you, create a playlist for your revision lessons, preferably with instrumental music. Avoid tunes with lyrics as they may distract you from focusing and concentrating. Choose something that will enhance your ability to stay focused; something relaxing and calming.

- Ensure revision is easy and accessible by keeping revision guides in visible locations such as next to your bed, by the toilet, or in the car. Remember, if the revision guides are out of sight, they are out of mind.

- Give yourself a treat while you are revising. For instance, after every 10 minutes of revision completed, reward yourself with a sweet or chocolate, if that brings you joy. It could be a colourful Skittle, a nutty M&M, or any other treat that takes your fancy.

REVISE LIKE THE GREATEST STUDENT IN THE WORLD

- Phones are amazing and fascinating pieces of technology, but they can also be very distracting. Therefore, it is important to keep your phone out of sight while you are revising. Once you have completed an hour of revision or achieved your set goal, go have some fun for 10 or so minutes.

- Take advantage of all revision or intervention sessions offered. Use this time to practice what you have learned in class, become better at solving problems, answering exam questions, and ultimately achieving better grades.

- What comes after daytime? Night. What comes after summer? Autumn. Easy, right?
  What comes after revising hard for your assessments? Success.

REVISE LIKE THE GREATEST STUDENT IN THE WORLD

- Why should you keep reminding yourself to revise? It is crucial to constantly remind yourself why you are investing the time and effort into revising. By doing so, you can set yourself up for success and achieve the best possible results.

- Achieve Your Best: By dedicating yourself to revising, you are creating an opportunity to reach your full potential academically. Through thorough understanding and practice, you will be able to perform at your highest level in exams and assessments.

54

READ SOMETHING NEW EVERY DAY

READ SOMETHING NEW EVERY DAY

- Read something new every day and you will learn something new every day.

- When you wake up in the morning, you have a very simple choice to make: Will you choose to have an amazing day and work hard towards future success, or not?

- Dreams don't come true while you are sleeping, so don't spend all your time in bed. Get up, work hard, and start learning, so you can start living the dream life you want - your best life.

- You are the only one in the universe who can control your future and your own life. So, what are you going to do today to ensure you have the future you want? Make the right decisions today.

READ SOMETHING NEW EVERY DAY

- Use the car, the bus, the tram, or the train as a mobile classroom. Take advantage of the time, whether it's just 5, 10, 15, or 20 minutes, to learn, to read, and to improve yourself. Don't waste this valuable time by watching other people on social media. They aren't concerned about you, so don't waste your time on them. Focus on yourself and prioritise learning.

- Take advantage of extra lessons when they are offered to you. Doing so will increase your knowledge, boost your confidence, and enable you to achieve excellent grades.

- No one is better than you, and no one is smarter than you. If other people in your class are being taught the same content as you, in the same classroom, by the same teachers, you can also achieve better grades. Nothing is stopping you from achieving excellent grades, is there?

READ SOMETHING NEW EVERY DAY

- When you find yourself in class, feeling distracted and disinterested, try saying the following phrase to help snap out of it: "I no longer wish to be this person anymore and I am determined to make a positive change in my life."

- What could you achieve if you have a phenomenal day today, tomorrow, and every day moving forward? You are truly capable of extraordinary things.

- Your phone could be costing you thousands of pounds every year. How? Well, consider this. The time you spend on your phone, watching, to be honest, mindless entertainment and nonsense, could have been better spent on your education. Investing that time in your education can ultimately help you earn more money in the future.

READ SOMETHING NEW EVERY DAY

- Enjoy the holidays: It's important to take time off and relax during the holidays. But, make time for reading. Even though you're on a break, try to dedicate at least 15 minutes a day to reading revision books. Keeping your brain engaged by reading during the holidays will help keep your brain active and prepared for the upcoming term and ultimately your future. By investing just this small amount of time in learning during your break, you'll have an advantage over students who neglect their studies.

- You can learn anything you want and achieve the goals you have set for yourself. This is a remarkable truth - there are no limits to what you can achieve. You are the only one who has the power to hold yourself back.

READ SOMETHING NEW EVERY DAY

- It doesn't matter how long it takes to get there; work hard every day until you do.

- You are always learning: at school, in your career, and your personal life. So, start early and become a great learner.

ALWAYS BE LEARNING

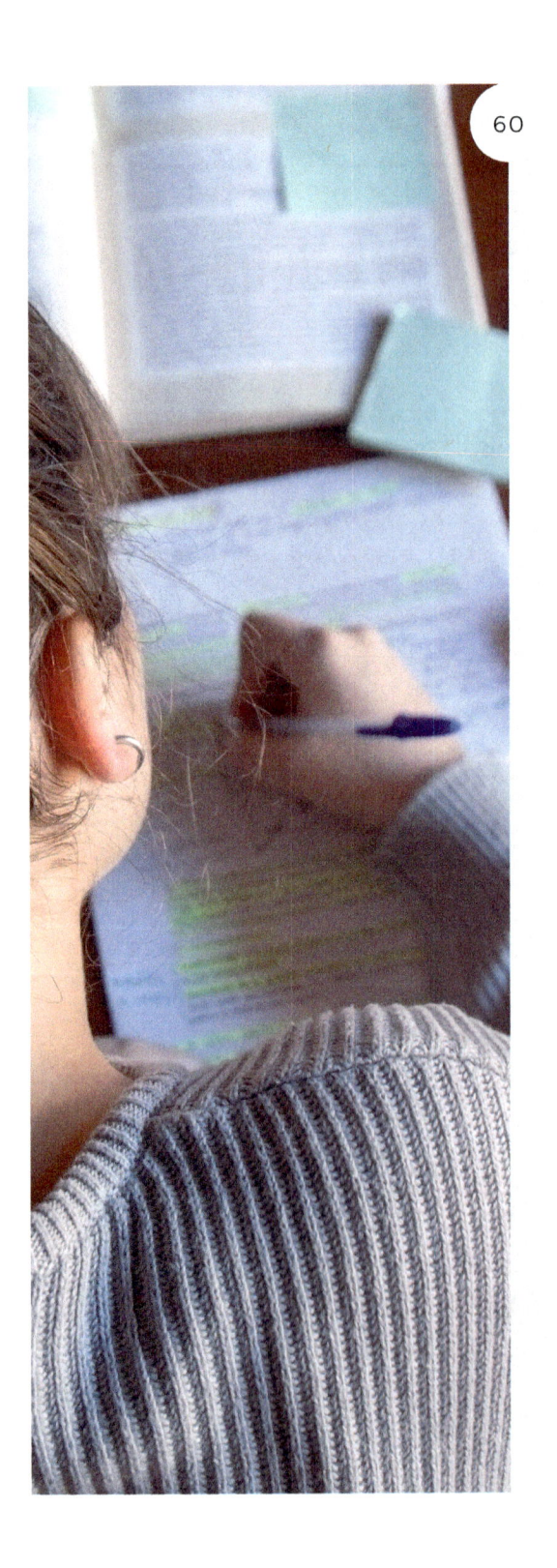

ALWAYS BE LEARNING

- Engage in home learning; yes, I said home learning, not homework - every night, especially if you haven't been assigned any. Begin by dedicating just five minutes to each subject you have studied on that particular day. You can simplify this by searching for five-minute educational videos on YouTube, watching them, and gaining a clearer understanding of what you have learned. This will give you an edge over your classmates and increase your chances for success in the future.

- Think of home learning as independent learning. This will make you a better learner and much more capable and skilled in your future tests, assessments, and exams; in other words, it will help you become the best version of yourself.

- Remember the saying, "Repetition Is Key?" - consistent practice leads to mastery.

ALWAYS BE LEARNING

- Take advantage of any home learning clubs offered to you. Use this time to ask questions, focus on your independent learning skills, and prioritise becoming better, if not brilliant in each subject. Ultimately, strive for improved grades and develop as a learner.

- Home learning prepares you for the next lesson. This is always the best way to approach a lesson - prepared and knowledgeable. The best preparation for tomorrow is to do superbly well today.

- Home learning will help you to navigate your way through this world and develop skills to become an independent thinker and a successful person.

- Develop this skill forever, after education, during your career, completing work, home or self projects; become a brilliant learner and organiser.

ALWAYS BE LEARNING

- Home learning is boundless because it is flexible and can be done anywhere. Whether you're in the car, on the bus, at the dining room table, or even on the toilet, you have the freedom to choose where you learn.

- Always prioritise your home learning, even if you find it challenging due to other obligations in the evening. These commitments may include taking care of siblings, assisting parents or carers, participating in sports clubs, dance sessions, or any other activities. If you struggle to allocate time in the evenings, consider waking up 15 minutes earlier in the morning to complete your tasks. This simple adjustment will help you solve the problem and ensure you make time for your home learning.

ALWAYS BE LEARNING

- Home learning provides an opportunity for you to review and reinforce your learning. Reflect on your understanding of the topic and how you found it. Engage in regular practice to become proficient in your work.

- Being committed to your home learning will improve your memory skills. When you learn and understand a topic, it is highly unlikely for it to become unfamiliar to you.

- Home learning encourages you to use your time wisely. Time management is a key requirement and skill for every job. So, plan your time effectively by making time for yourself, your family, and your friends. Additionally, remember to allocate time for your work as well; it will be beneficial in the long run.

ALWAYS BE LEARNING

- Home learning allows you to delve deeper into subjects beyond the limits of classroom time. While your teachers are incredible and possess extensive knowledge in their subjects, they cannot give you all their remarkable expertise. Therefore, investing time and effort into finding out new information for yourself is crucial. Always remember "The Universe is *such* a beautiful place, but so much more beautiful to know and understand".

- Home learning teaches students to take responsibility for their work. While teachers, friends, parents, and carers can provide guidance and support, it is ultimately the student's responsibility to complete their work and strive for success. Home learning serves as a valuable opportunity for students to contribute positively to their achievements.

ALWAYS BE LEARNING

- Home learning helps in the development of positive learning and study skills that will serve you well throughout your life. Learning is a lifelong process, even after leaving school and completing your education. It is important to strive to learn something new every day to succeed in your chosen career. Continuous learning is necessary to improve and progress in your field; otherwise, there is a risk of falling behind. Even I, Richard Whitaker, consider myself a student who learns something new every day. Why, you may ask? The answer is simple: to enhance my personal growth and to better myself.

- Home learning teaches you to work independently. Teachers can't hold your hand, while parents or carers can only do so for a limited time. We can certainly guide you in the right direction, but not forever.

ALWAYS BE LEARNING

- Home learning offers a valuable opportunity to broaden your knowledge and apply newfound skills to real-world situations. As you progress through your educational journey, you will develop the high-level skill of applying your knowledge. While teachers provide essential tools and guidance for understanding various subjects, it is impossible to cover every circumstance or scenario within a classroom setting. By dedicating time to further develop this skill at home, you can improve your practical application, which will most definitely prove beneficial in your chosen career and empower you as a problem solver throughout your life.

ALWAYS BE LEARNING

- When you are working; whether it is on your homework, a personal project or business project, remember this 'Golden Rule'; focus on this and nothing else. No phone calls, no messages, no social media, no visitors, no TV, no nothing. For this one, two or three hours of the day, this is your priority, this is the most important thing in the world, this attitude is the only way to living your life vision.

- Home learning fills your mind with wonderful knowledge and understanding, which helps you prepare for the future world. Knowing just a little bit about a lot of things will make you a much more interesting person in the future.

DON'T ACT LIKE AN IDIOT

DON'T ACT LIKE AN IDIOT

- It is our attitude towards the world and everyone in it that will determine other people's attitudes toward us. Nice things happen to nice people.

- No one wakes up in the morning, looks in the mirror, and says, 'I am an idiot. I'm going to act like an idiot and annoy everyone I meet.' No one likes an idiot, so be nice and kind to people; don't be an idiot.

- People who make foolish decisions and behave irresponsibly now will likely continue to do so in the future. On the other hand, individuals who work hard, are kind, respectful, and treat others with niceness now are more likely to experience happiness and success in the future.

- You don't always get what you want, you don't always get what you desire; you get what you deserve.

DON'T ACT LIKE AN IDIOT

- Smiling is contagious. Everyone wants to be happy, so take care of yourself, your health, your friends, and your family. Smile at people, be kind to others, and they will smile back.

- Smile at people, open the door for someone, or make a drink for a family member without being asked. Remember, nice things happen to nice people.

- Treat yourself like you would like to be treated. Being kind to others is a wonderful way to live, but it starts with liking yourself first.

- Liking yourself is important. The more you like yourself, the more likely other people are to like you. When you have a positive self-image, you will be happier, and this happiness will spread to others, creating a happier environment for everyone.

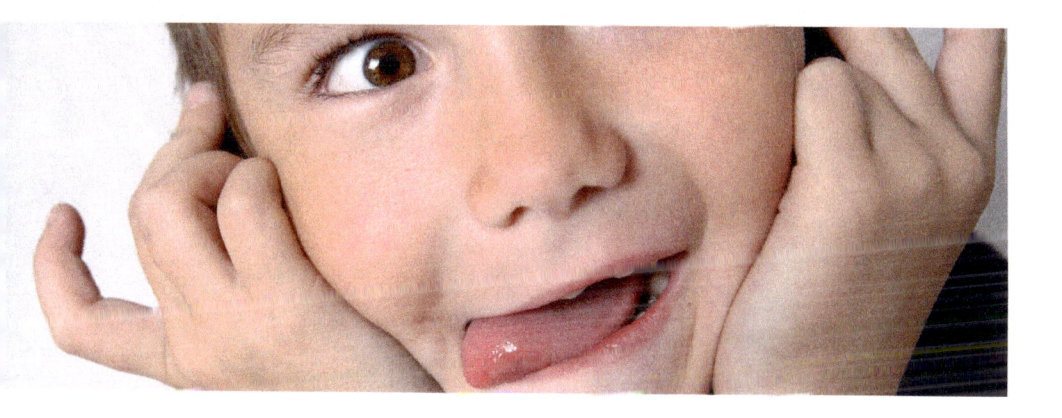

DON'T ACT LIKE AN IDIOT

- If you are unsatisfied with the grades you are achieving in your assessments, make changes to your approach. By being willing to make positive changes, you will see an improvement in your grades. Just like it is easy to change the radio station in the car, it can be just as easy as adjusting your study habits or seeking additional support.

- You are the only one who can create your thoughts, so bear this in mind and ask yourself this question: What are you thinking about most of the time? Stupid, silly, wasteful thoughts or thoughts of a successful and happy winner.

- The big question you need to ask yourself is, "What am I going to start doing differently today that will change my life for the better, tomorrow, and for the rest of my life?

DON'T ACT LIKE AN IDIOT

- When you improve, everything else improves. Therefore, attend your lessons punctually, concentrate on your work, strive to do your best, submit your homework promptly, revise for your tests, and treat everyone you encounter with kindness and respect.

- A quitter never wins, a winner never quits. So never quit.

- Please don't grow up stupid and skint. Attend school with determination, focus on learning, and strive for greatness.

74

WHAT I WISH I KNEW WHEN I WAS YOUR AGE

WHAT I WISH I KNEW WHEN I WAS YOUR AGE

- Speak up when something is on your mind: If you are upset, or worried about something, it is essential to talk to someone about it. Remember, there are plenty of people in your establishment who are there for you, even if you simply need someone to hear you out. Bottling up your emotions will only intensify your concerns and make things more challenging. However, rest assured, you will overcome whatever you are facing.

- When you are unsure about a topic or subject you are studying, make sure you ask someone for help. Ask your teacher; that's what they are there for. You can also ask a family member or a friend for assistance. Don't hesitate to reach out and seek guidance from someone.

WHAT I WISH I KNEW WHEN I WAS YOUR AGE

- **The best preparation for tomorrow is to do exceptionally well today. If you want to feel fully awake tomorrow, ensure you get a restful night's sleep tonight. If you want to perform well on your test tomorrow, dedicate time to revise today. If you want to feel fantastic and energetic tomorrow, make healthy food choices today. If you want to be appreciated tomorrow, show kindness towards others today.**

- **Spend time with people who consistently achieve good grades. Their positive attitude towards education and commitment to excellence will inspire and influence you positively.**

- **The more you know, the less you don't know. Simple, right? So, pick up a book, read, learn and ultimately become a more knowledgable and interesting person.**

WHAT I WISH I KNEW WHEN I WAS YOUR AGE

- **Appreciate that everyone is different.** People can have different opinions, so be open to listening to other people's views. You don't always have to agree, just be courteous.

- **Choose your friends wisely.** The people you choose to surround yourself with will ultimately shape the person you become in the future. Consider how your friends behave in class; if they tend to be disruptive, you will likely be too. Likewise, if your friends get in trouble in and out of school, you may find yourself getting involved too. Whether it's smoking, vaping, or achieving poor grades, your friends' habits can influence your own. Reflect on your friendships and ask yourself this important question: Would you want your future children to copy their behaviour at school or when out socialising? If the answer is no, then it may be time to make some changes.

WHAT I WISH I KNEW WHEN I WAS YOUR AGE

- Listening is more important than speaking; learn to become an amazing listener and show an interest in other people. Take an interest in what other people have to say, rather than making it just about yourself; people will like you a lot more. By doing this, you will be amazed at the number of true, amazing friends you will make and the amount of respect you will receive from others.

- Small changes can lead to significant transformations over time, so it's important to be patient. Begin improving your work ethic today, and you will be amazed by your future outcomes.

- It doesn't matter if you like the subject or not, or if you get along with the person sitting next to you or the teacher in front of you in the classroom. You still must do the very best you can, with no excuses, because it is your future. Don't let others affect your future.

WHAT I WISH I KNEW WHEN I WAS YOUR AGE

- By dedicating just one extra hour of study each day, either before or after school, you will elevate yourself from being average to significantly above average. Don't you aspire to be more than just average?

- What other people think about you is not as important as what you think about yourself. Ignore the haters, disregard the negative people, and concentrate on the positive.

- If you have fantastic self-esteem (if you like yourself), it won't bother you when someone says something nasty to you. Always remember that because you like yourself, you know deep down inside that you won't let their words hurt you.

WHAT I WISH I KNEW WHEN I WAS YOUR AGE

- Surround yourself with optimistic people who strive for success, rather than spending time with individuals who constantly complain and are full of negative thoughts and energy. Being around them will only bring you down and lead you towards an unhappy lifestyle, just like those people.

- When you improve, everything improves; therefore life improves and everyone's life around you.

- Whether you are at school, college, or university, education is a serious matter that can significantly impact your future. Therefore, it is essential not to underestimate the value of this incredible opportunity. Make the most of it, strive for excellence, complete your education, and make way for a fulfilling, prosperous, and joyful life ahead.

A NEW YOU

A NEW YOU

- Reach out to someone who is having a difficult day, engage in a conversation with them, listen to their concerns, and offer support to uplift their spirits. The positive impact you have on their well-being will leave you with an incredible sense of fulfilment.

- If you find yourself struggling with revision, pick up a revision guide and read it for five minutes. Five minutes is a great starting point. The next day, increase it to 10 minutes, and then to 15 the following day, and so on. Begin at a slow pace and gradually increase it.

- Next time you are struggling with a piece of work in class or at home, instead of just giving up or putting your head on the desk, ask someone for help and support. Get out of the habit of just giving up, become resilient; do not give up at the first sign of hardship.

A NEW YOU

- Give yourself extra homework every night, even if it is just fifteen minutes. You won't believe the positive impact it will have on your grades.

- Take extra pride in everything you do. This includes the way you complete your work, the way you talk to other people, the way you speak to yourself, and the way you present yourself. People will take notice, and this will propel you towards an incredible future.

- Exercise every day, even if it's just walking for an extra fifteen minutes. Do some press-ups, do some star jumps, and do some squats; do something every single day. Your body, your mental health, and your future self will be so grateful.

- Make sure to get outside more often. Take advantage of the sunshine and wrap up warm when it's cold. It's important to get fresh air every day, breathe in oxygen, and appreciate the beauty of the world around you.

A NEW YOU

- Take time away from your phone each day: Make sure to allocate a specific amount of time each day to step away from your phone, and no; during the night when you are asleep doesn't count, so no cheating. During this chosen time, ask someone to take care of your phone and keep it away from you. Utilise this valuable time to prioritise your well-being instead of focussing on others.

- Reach out to someone you haven't spoken with recently by making a phone call or sending them a message. Inquire about their well-being and ask about their friends and family. It's crucial to show care and concern for others, as we all require love and attention.

- Smile at people and be nice to them every day. Enjoy the positive impact you have on their feelings.

- Write down your goals every day and take action towards them every single day until you achieve them.

A NEW YOU

- Read something new every day; learn something new every day. Discover your interests, find joy, experience pleasure, and be inspired. Seek out a book on a topic that brings you happiness, and thoroughly enjoy reading your book.

- Make someone a drink without being asked. Do the washing up without being asked. Cook dinner without being asked. Look after your loved ones; make them feel loved and special.

- Perform random acts of kindness for your friends and teachers. Not only will this bring a smile to their face and yours, it will also make you feel amazing.

- Follow these straightforward actions consistently for an entire month, and prepare to be amazed by the outcomes. Not only will you experience a fantastic shift in your mindset, but you will also undergo a complete transformation; a new you.

GET A GREAT NIGHT'S SLEEP

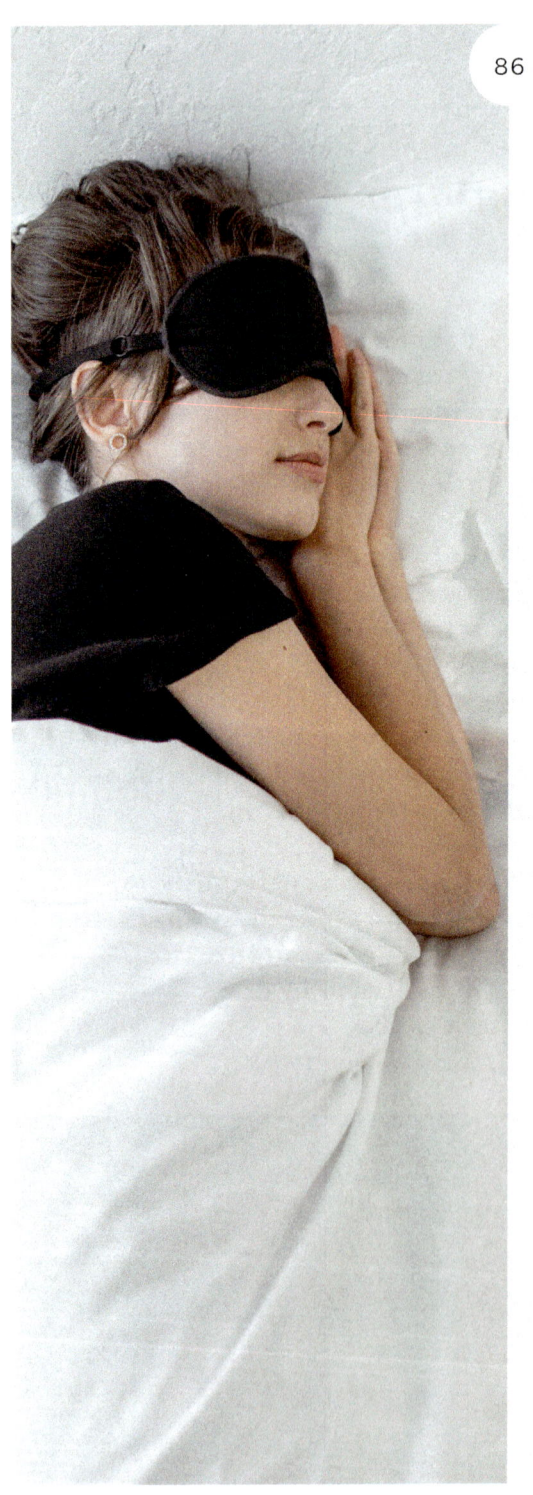

GET A GREAT NIGHT'S SLEEP

- Ensure you spend quality time with loved ones. They are the most important people in the world.

- Be prepared for tomorrow by laying out your clothes and packing your bag. Avoid finding yourself rushing around in the morning searching for your PE kit, homework, or tie. Being prepared is important.

- Tidy your room. You don't want to wake up to chaos in the morning or the smell of dirty socks. A tidy room equals a tidy mind. When you are tidy and organised, your life will have more purpose, and you can then focus and get on with the important stuff.

- Make sure you stretch for 5 to 10 minutes each evening. This will relieve any tension you have in your muscles and could improve your blood flow as well. Both of these benefits will help you relax and promote better sleep.

GET A GREAT NIGHT'S SLEEP

- Take a warm shower about an hour before bedtime. This will help lower your core temperature and improve the quality of your sleep. As a result, you will wake up refreshed in the morning and be ready to tackle the day ahead.

- To ensure productivity and a good night's sleep, I recommended that you create a to-do list before going to bed. By doing so, you will experience two significant benefits. Firstly, clearing your mind of upcoming tasks will enable you to sleep more soundly. Secondly, your subconscious mind will actively start working through the list, allowing you to work more efficiently and effectively the next day.

- Reflect on your day: How did it go? What went well? What didn't go well? What would you do differently next time if you could relive that day? Always improve the way you do things.

GET A GREAT NIGHT'S SLEEP

- Write down your goals. What do you want out of life? How do you want your life to look when you are older? Write them down on a piece of paper and place them next to your bed. This will be the first thing you see in the morning. Avoid looking at your phone first thing, ensuring you focus on yourself and not others; it is you that matters.

- Brush your teeth every night; no excuses. Take care of your teeth; there is nothing worse than toothache. Make sure to thoroughly remove any decaying food or bacteria to prevent it from festering overnight.

- To reduce the temptation of using your phone throughout the night, place it on the opposite side of the room. Alternatively, consider buying an alarm clock to wake you up in the morning, then you can keep your phone in a separate room.

GET A GREAT NIGHT'S SLEEP

- Make sure your room is as dark as possible. Turn off all screens, draw the curtains, and if available, use blackout blinds. Allow your mind to relax with minimal light.

- Consistent bedtime: Establish a regular time to go to bed, and your mind and body will adapt to a healthy sleep routine. Aim for a solid, uninterrupted 8 hours of sleep for optimal rest and rejuvenation.

- For the last 5 minutes before you sleep, use this time to compliment yourself. Remind yourself of how great you are, how hardworking you are, and how much you like yourself. Yes, I know, I get it, it may sound a bit silly at first, but so what. Start off by saying it quietly to yourself, get used to it, enjoy it, laugh at yourself; laughing is good. When you become an 'expert' at self-loving' shout it out... make sure you don't wake anyone up though lol.

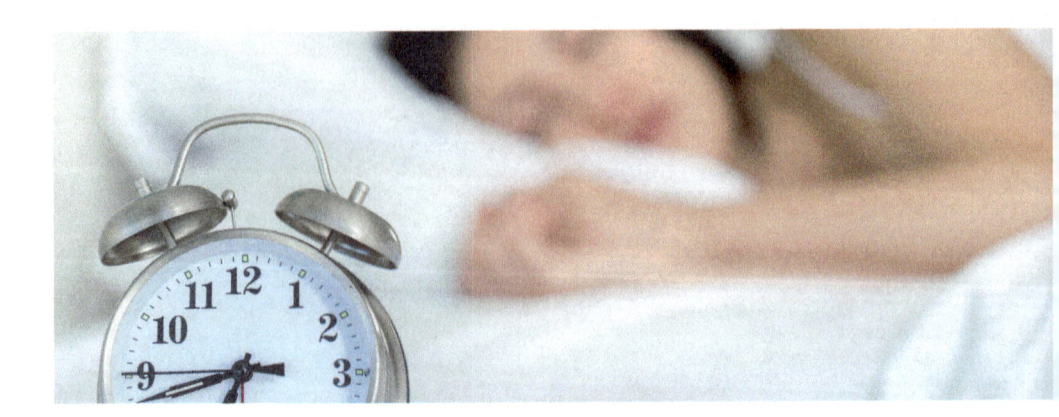

GET A GREAT NIGHT'S SLEEP

- If feasible, try to listen to a positive recording before falling asleep, such as a pre-recorded session or something from YouTube. This will help fill your subconscious mind with positive affirmations. When you wake up in the morning, not only will you feel great, but you will also feel positive and prepared for the day.

- Sleep well: Get a good night's sleep each night, and you will wake up feeling amazing and ready to make the most of each day.

FINAL THOUGHTS...

FINAL THOUGHTS...

- Dreams don't come true while you are sleeping, so don't spend all your time in bed. Get up, work hard, and start learning so you can start living the dream life you want; your best life.

- You do not have to be defined by your past. If you have made mistakes, hurt others, behaved poorly, or struggled in previous assessments, you have the power to make a change. You can choose to change for the better. Therefore, start your journey towards positive change today.

- It is often the kids who work the hardest and achieve excellent grades in school who tend to be the most successful and fulfilled in their future lives. It is not typically the class clown who reaches these levels of success.

- To achieve excellent grades, it is essential to excel in your learning. Therefore, it is important to begin building excellence in your learning habits.

FINAL THOUGHTS...

- While you are lying in bed, watching hours upon hours of videos on TikTok, Instagram, etc., there are lots of other people your age who are revising or doing some other kind of work. The sad reality is that you will both be applying for the same jobs when you leave education. Who's going to get that job that you want?

- When you leave education, you will need to continue educating yourself. If you are not actively improving, then in essence, you are going backwards. So, it is important to develop good habits from now on. Aim to become a lifelong learner, as it will be challenging in the future if you neglect this aspect.

- If you are unsure of the direction you are heading in life, simply ask yourself the following question: "How will things turn out for me if I continue doing what I am currently doing?"

FINAL THOUGHTS...

- Choose a book instead of watching a video on YouTube when you want to learn something. Books offer a distraction-free environment, whereas YouTube has many distractions. Focus on the task at hand, and once you have completed that task, you can enjoy and entertain yourself.

- You go to lessons to work, not to play. There are appropriate times in the day to play and have fun; lessons are not one of those times. Yes, of course, enjoy it, but stay focussed.
So, go and have fun at break time, playtime, or dinner time, not in the classroom.

- Being educated is not just about the grades you achieve; it is about how you develop your mind to attain whatever you desire. So, begin at a young age and become an amazing, confident learner.

FINAL THOUGHTS...

- Your future employers are not only interested in the grades you achieve throughout your time in education, although, of course, this matters a great deal. What also impresses them is who you are - the confidence you carry, the character you possess, and your personality. Ask yourself this question: if you were the boss of a big company, would you employ yourself? Be serious and honest with yourself when answering this question.

- Whether you are in school, college, or university, it doesn't matter. These are not just places you go to get an education; they are places where you can strive for the highest grades, providing you with the best opportunities in life and opening doors to numerous career paths.

FINAL THOUGHTS...

- A person who can read but chooses not to is no better off than a person who cannot read at all. Therefore, it is important to make the most of this ability. Improve yourself and strive to learn something new each day.

- You own your thoughts, so remember to fill your mind with happy, successful, positive, and rich thoughts, not sad, unsuccessful, negative, and poor thoughts.

- Now go out there and become 'The Greatest Student in The World'.

NOTES & DOODLES...

NOTES & DOODLES...

NOTES & DOODLES...

NOTES & DOODLES...

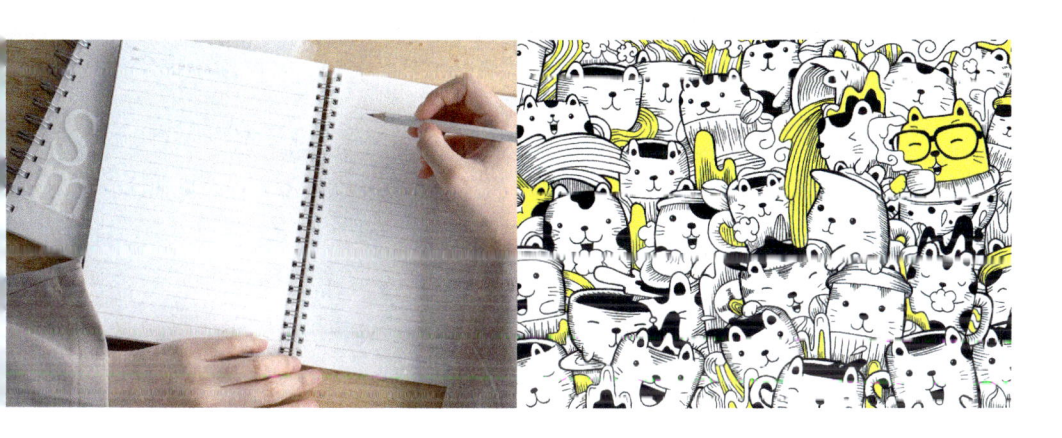

ABOUT THE AUTHOR

Firstly, I would like to personally thank you ever so much for reading my book; it means a great deal that you have taken time out of your busy lives. I sincerely hope it has been an eye-opener and helps you become 'The Greatest Student in The World', not just during your studying days but also throughout your life. May your life be happy, successful, and full of love.

ABOUT THE AUTHOR

After running bars and clubs in Leeds and the North of England for a decade, I decided to pursue higher education. At the age of 31, I enrolled in The University of Leeds to study Physics with Astrophysics. Four years later, I successfully graduated with a 2:1 with Honours and subsequently pursued my PGCE certification. My teaching journey started at the age of 36, and over the past 16 years, I have not only taught, mentored and supported students but also fellow educators. As an educator, I find immense joy in motivating and inspiring young minds, while also exploring the intricacies of psychology and the human mind. I am an avid reader, always striving to learn something new every day through my regular reading habits.

OTHER GREAT BOOKS FOR YOUR LIBRARY

Just a few of the books I have read, enjoyed and learnt from. These have had a massive influence on me, my life and in writing this book.

Think and Grow Rich (Napoleon Hill)

The 5am Club (Robin Sharma)

Eat That Frog (Brian Tracy)

7 Strategies for Wealth & Happiness Jim Rohn)

How to Win Friends and Influence People (Dale Carnegie)

Key Person of Influence (Daniel Priestley)

Start With Why (Simon Sinek)

Notes from a Friend (Anthony Robbins)

The 4-Hour Week (Timothy Ferriss)

How Successful People Think (John C Maxwell)

A PUBLIC THANK YOU

I could never have done this without you; thank you.

Laura (Very beneficial for me)
Amazing book which was super easy to read and had a lot of information! Really helped me out and I hope it can help so many others out too!
10/10 recommend :)

Aimee (Packed full of information)
This book is laid out clearly and the bullet points make it easy to read and take in, especially for students who do not enjoy to read!! I would recommend this book to anybody looking for some motivation in their life to achieve their goals!♥

Noë + Madeline (111/5 ★)
Greatest book of all time , would recommend to any parents for their children class book for such a reasonable price, easy read and the most interesting thing I've read in a long while.

A PUBLIC THANK YOU

I could never have done this without you; thank you.

Paul Proctor (Greatest student in the world 🖤)
I purchased this book for my daughters but decided to read it myself first, i have enjoyed reading this book it is to the point and uncomplicated in its direction in an easy to follow format it Helps the reader to prioritise and organise one's life goals and objectives often books tend to overcomplicate and glamorise the A to Z of success not this one what I like most about this book is that it encourages everyone to go ahead and be the best version of you for you.
Well done Author 👏

Carl R (A Must Have For All Ages!!)
From start to finish this book provides the stepping stones for anyone to become clear minded, self believing, and helps build your successful future with very easy to follow guidance....
I'm looking forward to the next installment from this brilliant life skills teacher....

A PUBLIC THANK YOU

I could never have done this without you; thank you.

Stephen (Excellent book from a High School parent perspective.)
This is a really good, well thought out book for students especially those that don't like long drawn out books and get bored easily. (I have one of these!)
It isn't too long, great font size, good ratio of words to pictures, everything ticks the box for students and is a good read all round to make anyone re think and evaluate their life.

Dave Dawson (A must read!)
This book is thoughtfully constructed, yet easy to read and follow. Great insights and a must read. Exceptional learning tool. Highly recommended 🔥 Will help and guide students of all ages. Great experience 👍

Sandy Gill (Teenage Daughter loved it!)
It gave my daughter great ideas and confidence to tackle the year ahead. Would recommend to any student great motivational book.

A PUBLIC THANK YOU

I could never have done this without you; thank you.

Stuart Keith (Excellent 10/10)
What a great read. Full of motivational and inspirational ideas. My daughters loved reading it, and this book will definitely help them do amazing at school.

Joanne McCann (The Greatest Student in the World)
I think anyone could take something from this book not just students!
Great motivational book! X

Debbie (Amazing and full of inspiration)
This book is full of useful and insightful help for students. My daughter is just about to choose her options and found it really helpful. It is well written and not too long. Well worth the money and read ●

Steve D (Inspirational Read)
Really enjoyed reading this book, I found it very motivating and like the individual short sections. A great read for younger students ●

A PUBLIC THANK YOU

I could never have done this without you; thank you.

Clive Newman
Fantastic book. Pitched at the appropriate level to be informative, succinct, and a great educational tool. Although I bought this for my child, there is material I can take from it - from a learning and development aspect.

Rich (A must read for all students, teachers and parents)
Easy to read and so much information in there. This book is not just for students but also anyone who wants happiness and success.

Deborah Fisher (Encouragement)
I bought this book for my daughter to give her some positive thoughts & she absolutely loved it!
And now my 15year old son has decided he'd also like to read it something he never does & said he's enjoying it.

Yasmin (Great Book!!)
Really helps.

A PUBLIC THANK YOU

I could never have done this without you; thank you.

Amazon Customer (Inspiring Book)
A really great read, I bought this book for my son who is doing his A levels, he found it incredibly motivating and inspiring. Highly recommend!

Amazon Customer (Fantastic Book)
Got this book for my son, he thinks the book is very insightful and interesting. Very happy with the purchase thank you.

Would you like to appear in my next addition? Simply leave a nice review and I will gladly add you to this list of amazing people. Thank you and may your life be full of happiness and success.

Printed in Great Britain
by Amazon